A Lesson for Martin Luther King Jr.

written by **Denise Lewis Patrick**

illustrated by **Rodney S. Pate**

Aladdin

New York   London   Toronto   Sydney   Singapore

For my mother and father. —D. L. P.

To Dr. M L King and Dr. M G Davey. —R. S. P.

First Aladdin edition December 2003

Text copyright © 2003 by Denise Lewis Patrick

Illustrations copyright © 2003 by Rodney S. Pate

ALADDIN PAPERBACKS

An imprint of Simon & Schuster Children's Publishing Division

1230 Avenue of the Americas, New York, NY 10020

Book design by Lisa Vega

The text of this book was set in Century Old Style.

Printed in the United States of America

2 4 6 8 10 9 7 5 3

Library of Congress Cataloging-in-Publication Data

Patrick, Denise Lewis.

A Lesson for Martin Luther King Jr. / by Denise Lewis

Patrick ; illustrated by Rodney S. Pate.

p. cm. — (Ready-to-read) (Childhood of famous Americans)

Summary: Relates an incident from the childhood of civil rights leader

Martin Luther King Jr., when his best friend's father said they could no longer

play together because "colored and white can't mix."

ISBN 0-689-85397-1 (Aladdin pbk.) — ISBN 0-689-85398-X (Aladdin Library edition)

1. King, Martin Luther Jr., 1929–1968—Childhood and youth—Anecdotes—

Juvenile literature. 2. Friendship—United States—Anecdotes—Juvenile literature.

3. Racism—United States—Anecdotes—Juvenile literature.

4. African Americans—Biography—Anecdotes—Juvenile literature.

[1. King, Martin Luther Jr., 1929–1968—Childhood and youth. 2. Friendship. 3. Racism.

4. Civil rights workers. 5. African Americans—Biography.] I. Pate, Rodney, ill. II. Title.

III. Series. IV. Childhood of famous Americans series.

E185.97.K5 P27 2002

323'.092—dc21

2002003209

A Lesson for
Martin Luther
King Jr.

It was a sunny, perfect
September afternoon.
Martin's first day of school
was over.
He was so excited!

He went across the road

to the grocery store

to tell his best friend all about it.

"Bobby, I have my very own
reading book.
Want to see?" Martin asked.
"Maybe later,"
Bobby said.

He seemed really busy

putting cans on a shelf.

Bobby's father owned the store.

Sometimes Bobby helped out.

"Can you play ball
when you finish?" Martin asked.
He and Bobby had spent the
whole summer throwing curveballs
and fastballs in the empty lot
next to the store.
Now they were going
to different schools.

"Maybe . . ."

Bobby grinned at Martin.

"Great!"
Martin went off
to do his homework.
But Bobby
didn't come over
to play that day
or the next.

On Friday Martin took
some of his mama's oatmeal cookies
to the store.
He shoved his baseball into his pocket
just in case.

"Hey!" Martin called.

He held out the cookies.

"I—I can't!"
Bobby said no before
Martin asked him anything at all!
Martin frowned
and slowly walked away.

That night Martin talked
to his big sister Christine.
"You think Bobby's mad at me?"

"No. Maybe his dad wants him to learn more about the store," she told him.

Martin decided
to ask Bobby
if this was true.
He watched from
his living room window
as the store closed.

16

When Bobby ran out

to get into his mother's car,

Martin ran out too.

"Bobby!" Martin called.

"My papa said I can't
play with you anymore!"
Bobby's face turned red.
"Why?" Martin asked.
"Because you are colored
and I am white, Martin.
Papa says colored and
white can't mix."

Martin watched the car drive off.

He didn't understand.

Later on at suppertime
Martin's father
had come home from work.
Everyone was at the table.

"What's this sad face, son?"
his father asked.
Martin put down his fork.
"Bobby's daddy told him
to quit playing with me
because I am not white."

"That's not fair!"
Christine talked and chewed
at the same time.

"No, it's not,"

Daddy said in a serious voice.

"Why does color

make any difference?" Martin asked.

"Well, some white folks believe
they are better than
we black people."

Mama nodded.

"So they treat colored people badly.
We can't eat in the same restaurants
or stay in the same hotels
as they do."

"And let me tell you, children,"
Daddy said,
"I do not like being treated differently
only because of the color of my skin."

Martin looked down at his plate.

He didn't feel like eating anymore.

But then he got an idea.

"Can't I change the rules?
Can't I change people's minds?"
he asked his father.
Daddy smiled.

"Yes, you can," he said.

"You may have lost a friend today.

But I want you to remember

that friendship has no color, Martin."

"I will try, Daddy,"

Martin said. "I will try."

Martin Luther King Jr. never forgot that hard lesson. He spent his life trying to change people's ideas about friendship and peace. He dreamed of living in a world where all people treat each other fairly. Today people in the U.S. and other countries work to make Dr. King's dream come true.

Here is a timeline of Dr. King's life.

1929   Born in Atlanta, Georgia, on January 15

1944   Began studies at Morehouse College,
        at age fifteen

1953   Married Coretta Scott;
        they later had four children

1955   Received a Ph.D. in theology,
        following his father and grandfather into the
        Baptist ministry

1955   Helped lead a bus boycott started by Rosa
        Parks against unfair bus laws in Montgomery,
        Alabama

1963   Marched on Washington and made his famous
        "I Have a Dream" speech from the steps of the
        Lincoln Memorial

1964   Awarded the Nobel Peace Prize,
        the youngest to ever receive the award

1968   Died in Memphis, Tennessee,
        on April 4, after being shot